I0203620

MURAL

POEMS BY
ALICE ELIZABETH ROGOFF

BLUE LIGHT PRESS ◆ 1ST WORLD LIBRARY

1st WORLD
LIBRARY
Literary Society

AUSTIN ◆ FAIRFIELD ◆ DELHI

MURAL

1ST WORLD LIBRARY

PO Box 2211, Fairfield, Iowa 52556
www.1stworldlibrary.com

BLUE LIGHT PRESS

PO Box 642, Fairfield, Iowa 52556

COVER, INTERIOR ART AND BOOK DESIGN:

Melanie Gendron

COVER ART:

By Anton Refregier, with assistance by Louise Gilbert, Rincon
Center, San Francisco, California
FRONT COVER: *Torchlight Procession (Picketing for the
Eight-Hour Day)*
BACK COVER: *Building the Railroad*
FRONT and BACK COVER PHOTOGRAPHS: courtesy of
Fred Glass and the Golden Lands, Working Hands Project
PHOTOGRAPHER: David Bacon

FIRST EDITION
ISBN: 1-59540-902-5

ACKNOWLEDGEMENTS

Some of these poems have previously appeared in this version or in a slightly different version in *Awaa-te* 4, *Baker Street Irregular, The Steelhead Special, Poetry USA* , the *Haight Ashbury Literary Journal, Gypsy Table, Gyst, Street Sheet, The View from Here, Vice & Verse, Paper Boat, Agua Caliente,* and *It's All Good.*

MURAL

TABLE OF CONTENTS

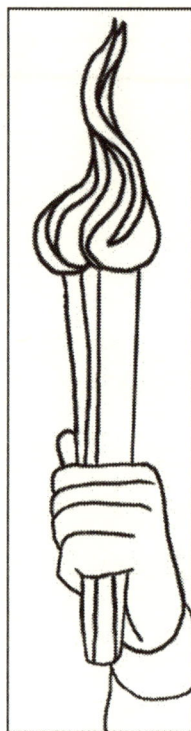

WHY A WORKERS' MURAL HANGS ON

At Rincon Annex, with paintings of labor,
the building's new owners
have made a post office into a mall
and don't want the murals there.
Paintings don't have souls.
They don't bleed when cut
or cry when they are painted over
but maybe, at Rincon Annex
the Chinese workers' ghosts would have
come downtown and then
hollered and shouted at the passing
tourists and Christmas shoppers.
The ghosts may materialize as one scurries away
with packages.
Maybe the Native Americans' drums
would be heard for miles,
and Tom Mooney's ghost would sing
prison songs with Joe Hill's and Harry Bridges',
the voices noisy, loud, and rowdy,
so loud that cars would beep
as they drove by,
the drivers waving their hands
in unity,
so maybe, that's why the
Rincon Annex murals got to stay.

PARC 55 VICTORY

Each hotel worker has
circled the hotel entrance
a hundred times;
each waiter and janitor
carries a sign
and shouts at the owner
sheltered far in the building;
their arms hurt a little
from the pickets;
the cooks and cleaners
have been singing
for an hour,
their songs on crumpled
sheets of paper,
folded many times.
They get the intangible things
they want when cars
drive by and honk.
The tourists are
flustered by the
noise and crowd;
they confusedly drive in
being asked by Arlene to leave.
The demonstration
has lasted two hours,
and it is getting to be dusk,
getting to be the
end of lunch hour,
or time to break up.

2

The circle has held.
When they sign her Union contract,
Arlene hugs Alice, Alice hugs Ricardo,
Ricardo hugs Felix,
Felix hugs Ella, Ella hugs David,
David hugs the next in line.

SOLIDARITY

The docks on the Pacific could be quiet
as sea shells today
as work stops for
the striking Dock Workers
in Liverpool;
the docks could also
reverberate like blown conches
across the ocean,
rings inside the shells
making one circle
spiraling into one vortex.
And a rusty crane slices
through the sky,
and the birds migrate
from one port to another.
No one's been talking
about Liverpool much,
the newspaper owners
don't tell you anything much.
Closing down the
West Coast Piers
will say a great deal.

THE DAY LABORERS

Day laborers
line Cesar Chavez Street,
a small group of men
on each corner,
workers
waiting
ready to go
or not,
getting by
until the next day;
the on-the-street hiring hall
where the INS
may show up,
or not;
another day
of Spanish-speaking men
looking.
I glide by inside
a car window
looking for
my day to begin.
We are all starting our day.
For the men on the corners,
each day starts
over and over
again.

FOR *THE CHRONICLE* CARRIER GIRLS AND BOYS

They're too young to have read
the Theory of Surplus-Value.
She's just been working hard,
delivering the papers,
working on her throw.
He's just a kid,
he's too young to know what
the Theory of Surplus-Value means,
he doesn't know why someone thinks
that he's a surplus, and the newspaper boys
and girls have to go.
He thinks a surplus is like an extra sack
of potatoes that gets tossed in a truck
and that gets shipped back
or is thrown away,
except he's ten, and she's eleven,
and unlike sacks
they breathe when they run
and when they laugh, when they
have a little money to take home.
A surplus, she thinks is like pairs
of old jeans in a store
on Mission Street,
except the newspaper girls and boys;
they breathe as they yell and as they cry
and they cry not to have their jobs;
and now little boys and girls are beginning
to understand how people can be
Surplus, too.

INTERNATIONAL WOMEN'S DAY

Cherry trees blooming
everywhere
through the fog,
loose weavings of
petals
throughout the City
of San Francisco,
aromas of blooming
burning bushes
blending their fragrances;
It is like a song
to me each spring,
the spring that brings
forth the faces of
women unfolding.

WORK-STOPPAGE

Mining
through solid rock,
to crack layers, one after
another;
The people
appear small
compared to the machines
that rhythmically break;
Silence of the machines
when the people strike
for freedom,
When the people stop
work stopping,
the torn earth
sleeping momentarily;
And one hears voices
as the machines stop pounding,
Voices for freedom
in the South African dust.

CHICAGO TRAFFIC

the wind has gotten
into my bones,
blowing off
the lake,
through the
crowds of people
pushing through
the loop,
the trains
whiz overhead,
spiraling
around
flattening
people against
each other.
the wind
makes me
feel angular,
as though
bones have
pierced
through my
skin,
rolling, rolling
through the
newest human
waves.

THE CHICAGO STOCKYARDS

go through the
old stockyards,
the ghosts of animals
live there
their bawling
fills the empty stalls,
other streets
don't intone
as much
as this one
does.

THE WORKMEN'S CIRCLE

Odd collection of stones,
gathered together in death,
like at a meeting,
an underground meeting of bones
sifting thoughts in
Brooklyn's dirt,
Silently gathered,
surely, all these organizers
would like to make a speech,
agitate for someone's rights,
perhaps, they are in an argument;
The meeting just goes on and on,
year by year,
through the spring rains
and falling leaves;
Surely, they must be late for dinner
or another appointment.

THE LAST ROLL OF FILM

I can't remember what was
the last roll of film
from our trip.
Then slowly,
like negatives appearing
in a wash,
the photos
materialize to me;
I am pointing
my camera
at Henry Moore's statue
to mark the discovery
of atomic fission,
and a bus of tourists
from Japan arrives,
and they point their cameras
at the statue, around it, on all sides,
and I visualize
my photos,
one side of the sculpture
like a helmet,
one side like a mushroom cloud,
one side like a skull,
my eyes improvising
on the shapes.
The tourists from Japan
photographed quickly
and returned to their bus,
but I ponderously recorded
the stone monument
that looks both
heavy and iridescently light.

NUCLEAR SOUND

I hear a cry in the night
A small sound
Cats in the trees
Fault lines
The desert intruding on the city
It lapping like oceans
A remembered sudden heat on my face
From a car's momentum
Through Nevada
The sound of an arrow,
No, a missile,
Pointing desolately
At the nuclear testing-
Ground – it's an arid
Sound,
Feels like shock.

THE CIVIL RIGHTS MEMORIAL
Montgomery, Alabama 1992

In the circle of water,
Crescents of the late falling
Leaves,
People quickly walking by,
Dr. King's church
A half a block away,
At lunchtime, it is quiet,
Each rectangle of stone
Another death, so
Quiet in death, now,
Each death flared
In violence like
A horse with fire
From its mouth,
An entire circle
More death than I had known,
On this quiet street
The Poverty Project building
Stands behind the Civil Rights Memorial
Like a big parent, and
One can easily
Smooth one's hands
And say
The Night Riders are gone now
And then the sun sets
The sun bleeding orange,
And then, the Klan
Reappears like a
Rotting sour horse
As the sun sets,
A bleeding circle
Of puce red.

THE MOANING GROVE

The eucalyptus speak –
The grove is a bellows,
The wind fueling their voices,
Come from afar,
Their eerie cries
A language that has yet
To be translated;
They now sound like babies
Lost on the shore
Of the pond.
Some people row closer
To listen to them;
Some people blame them
For fires, for droughts,
And never come closer
To hear them speak.

THE PRISONER

My baby, said the
prisoner, grew
inside me in
prison, illegally,
and born in
prison.
She imagined
her baby
crawling beneath
the bars and keys
that keep her in,
most of the women in prison locked up
for nonviolent crimes.
Her baby, she dreamed
crawling at the
foot of a tree
but beyond the tree
all she could see
was the hard prison floor.

MEXICO CITY

bone
and bread
and
market place of
life,

on the road
leading to the
center,

women with
white hair

women with
the backs of their
legs muscled

women carrying
babies wrapped
in a shawl,

all roads lead
to the center

market place of
sinewy tongues

the bone reaches
out of the
flesh

a fish is delivered
with a
knife

on the walls
of Frida's
heart
are paintings

all roads lead

to the center.

CURFEW
After the Rodney King Riots

The city is
very quiet
at curfew
with the dividing line
between day
and the time
when only the
howling sorts roam,
I feel naked
stepping from a car
to an art gallery –
most of the artists
are not going to be there;
I go inside like to
a warm fireplace,
step outside
because that's freedom,
dance back inside
glad that art still exists,
it feels like
the city has been covered
by a blanket
with a contagious disease.
Then I regroup
in the gathering
that continued to happen
despite the
curfew.

GRAVES

Going to the Jewish Hungarian cemetery,
I pick up rocks
to place on the graves
of my relatives;
there are very few rocks available
on the paths today,
like the crop has temporarily dwindled,
as though they had all been reaped,
or had not grown into harvest;
I gather enough for
each member of the family,
and set three small rocks
on each grave.
In the Middle East,
there are Palestinian graves
made of rocks,
and in my hands
I gently close my fingers
over the rocks
for the liberation of the living,
and for all of the dead.

INVISIBLE JOURNALISM

The Protest March started with
a row of veterans
Viet Nam veterans
and some veterans from World War II,
leading 100,000 marchers
across Market Street;
When I think of the weeks
surrounding the Gulf War
I see the television cameras
focused on these vets
seeking their parade
in the aftermath
of Iraq,
and the lenses turning
away from that picture –
of the veterans at the head
of the long 100,000 march to
protest war
and then, the banners
of labor,
and messages for world peace.
No interviews,
No slides, and negatives in a box.
I would like to enlarge
those faces and voices
that passed in front
of cameras
that had eyes closed
and made half tones
that bleed.

WILL WE REMEMBER THESE DEMONSTRATIONS?

On Haight Street
Politics run by
In a rush
Like a flash flood,
A deep anger
In the desert,
An angry burning
To the government. Then,
Another flash flood of
Bodies. A rainy season
In a drought.
Like the war, these bodies
Are quick,
And they end
With a flick
Like the tail
Of a snake.

KHADESH-BARNEA
Sinai Desert

boundaries in danger of war
souls tangled in moonlight
carved lanes through the desert
kisses extending towards each other
weapons like lions
lions' gates inviting entrance
calm quiet imaginary cities of the desert
the womb of the sheep
caressed with milk
the hand fondles the silky softness
the eyes of date trees wrestle with mountains.

exiles to retell the future
camels loaded with candles

oasis of time
oasis of time

the high voice of the mosque
the sky, purple harmony
our souls, barbed wire fantasia
white veils purest reality
the hands speaking with mountains.

surreal vision
the hand feeding figs and oranges
into the mouth of the moon
the tribes of the oasis

calling to those inscribed
in the book of life,
the calm quiet imaginary
cities of the desert
gathering in spirit forces.

our boundaries are
pressed upon and the hand
caresses the silky softness
brings out a lamb.

on four wobbly legs
the prince, the shepherd,
the king, the law-giver.

the calm quiet imaginary cities of the desert
our souls tangled in purest reality.

LAMENT FOR VIET NAM

Rice
Growing in
Wet land
Heart-land-aches
Spring rains wake
In morning
Monsoon soon
Wash away
Warm chill
Children gone
Gather crop
Wade in water
Wait for return
Wind sighs
Cycle
Revolves.

MATRIX

In the dictionary,
accidentally,
under the Ms,
I find the word *Matrix*.
The root of this word
is Mater, Mother.
It seems ironic;
In the *Unabridged
Universal Dictionary*,
Matrix has many meanings;
The first meaning of Matrix is
the womb, source, origin,
the womb which helps us grow,
protects us;
I continue to read
and the vocabulary lesson resumes:
Two: "That which encloses anything,"
perhaps, a closer definition
to the The Matrix Program,
which encounters the homeless,
and more definitions follow
in fine detail:
Three: "In typefounding, a bar of copper
having an impress of the punch,"
to impress – would it be to teach
or to seize?
Four: "In mineralogy, the rock or main
substance in which any accidental
crystal, mineral, or fossil is embedded."

In *Random House*, "In the circuit of an
electronic computer, an array of components
for translating from one code to another."

— Matrix Program —
What is its meaning?
Are you in a womb,
in an enclosure,
a component in a code,
or are you an accidental crystal?
    As shopping carts are taken,
    as blankets and photographs go,
    something is wrong with the vocabulary today,
The root of Matrix is Mater, Mother.
When a root dies,
what is next?

ARGOS

On the sidewalk
Lies the old dog waiting,
If only he were Odysseus' dog,
An Argos,
Seeing the thousands
Of homeless pass him by,
Returning home –
Recognizing all the old travelers,
Seeing through
Their rags,
Recognizing their
Translucent souls.

THE HERMIT CRAB

The hermit crab
has found a home
in an abandoned shell;
On a stretch of beach
the crab carries his new
home on his back
past an encampment
of people
who are told to move on,
who are told that
they have stayed too long,
while the crab inches
towards the tide,
being part of nature
knowing little of Property.

FOOD LINES

The lines are a daily occurrence,
Some people are there early for food,
Others arrive to take their place
At the end of a long line,
Some days the lines are quiet,
Other days, there is loud talk.
Teddy gets food every day,
Abby came for a month,
Others appear and
Disappear like smoke,
Sometimes there is rain or heat,
In Chicago and Boston and
New York, there is snow
That falls on the old shoulders
And young heads, and all the toes
Of the bodies that move
Through these lines;
One day, there is hope
In the lines,
On Wednesday, it is sadness,
Yesterday, a large woman in a raincoat
Sat in the line,
Some people remain
Alive because of the lines.

The lines of hungry people
Out of the Soup Kitchens
Have lasted for as many years
As for a young person to have grown up.

The name of this person
Is sometimes despair,
Sometimes it is love,
Sometimes it is sorrow,
Sometimes it is joy –
Sometimes Joy has
Her own children
Within the lines
That murmur
And sleep,
At noon,
In every American city,
The lines that
Do not subside.

ON THE STREET

There is only a thin towel around my shoulders
on a street corner without a name
I imagine that the towel has become a fur stole
that I saw around a lavender-scented woman
and I felt suddenly warm in the wind
from this rich pelt
Laughing to myself, I think
a lady has thrown hers onto me
and for the longest time, I can't feel
the wind, the rain, any kind of cold
until I feel so frightened
because I might be dead,
and it is snowing
and I am warm.
"I am dead," the brown mink says to me.
"I was forced to live in a closet,
but once I ran in the woods,"
and I look at the stole,
and it is alive.
It snuggles against my neck.
Then it sits at my feet
like a cat.
And then the kind live mink
goes where imaginary animals go,
And I sit on the street
with a towel on my shoulders
in the maddening wind and snow.

THE DOLPHIN

the dolphin
leaps, flashes,
primal memory
archetype of mystical voyages,
mythological islands,
the high songs of dolphins
like neurons
leaping through the
corridors of expansive
rooms upon rooms
in the houses of my dreams.
the dolphin is a gestalt,
reduced to flesh,
possible to crumble,
genetic memory in nets,
coursing through
the blood and brain stream
as screams,
mutilated,
dead dreams,
empty seas
lost of vision,
of harmonies as yet unheard.

AM I LIVING IN THE PAST?

Being an owl, I merely look for
a tree to land upon,
It is not the past I'm trying to find,
I do not fly towards the past,
just towards a hollow trunk,
except I keep bumping into
roofs
and new wood frames for people nests,
so I fly, fly, fly wide-winged into the night,
but bump into the present,
four new roofs.
If I were a stork
I'd stay and settle
on a chimney
but for a hundred thousand years
I have lived in trees
So, I fly fly fly
to find a present and
future forest,
even one,
just one,
before it is my wings and
the night,
and my future is my past.

THE SOUND OF A TREE GONE

The water falls and falls and falls,
Like the om in Tibetan ritual,
Its highs and lows,
Like a slit-drum,
The pond at the bottom,
Silent and serene,
Like a clear night,
And another sound of falling,
Further into the forest,
Sharp, quick, buzz, snap,
A rush of wind,
Hit, rumble,
The toppling of a great tree,
And stillness at the bottom,
But no continuity,
And only an empty night
As the tree is hauled, rattling, away.

ON THE WOODED ISLE

Her bird watchers traverse
The Wooded Isle each week.
My Mother-in-law has been
telling me about her
walks for years,
but finally we go there.
She takes David and me.
On the Chicago South Side
we drive on Stoney Island
along the Midway
and through the tunnel
passing the mural
of African-American heroes,
turn by the huge Museum
of Science and Industry,
and stop in front
of a little bridge.
Mildred, who is eighty-five
years old,
says we can get on the Island
in one of many ways –
over this bridge or another.
We take the first bridge,
enter a Japanese garden,
step across large stones
in a pond.
It is November,
that gray clear month,
a very cold month

for the Californians
of twenty years,
yet not too cold
for the constant Midwesterner.
We walk the stone path
and balance carefully
to not slip into the cold water,
after this day
Mildred will refrain
from crossing
these rocks.
One moment, we are
in Chicago,
the next moment,
we are someplace else,
someplace resurrected
from its historical
destruction.
During World War Two,
the garden was demolished.
My Mother-in-law describes
how it became a ruins,
as though it had been bombed
and left for dead.
Finally, it was restored,
the vines cleared,
the garden given breath,
allowed its tranquility,
statues and stones set aright.
There is a view across the larger lake,
and a small shrine,

the lure of possible birds to see,
a crane,
a clump of long grass,
the smooth rocks,
the garden's sad destiny.
My Mother-in-law
says there is another choice to make
to complete the walk around the Isle:
Straight across a meadow,
or on a dirt road in a circular route.
We choose the wide meadow,
and step over the stones again, leaving
the peaceful spot
whose pain still shows
around its unfinished edges,
and under a circle
on The Wooded Isle.

NEIGHBOR

Robert Frost,
The last to talk of neighbors.

It was empty land,
A lot owned by the city,
Flowers were planted
By a neighbor
Then more
It became a park,
I wanted to know
What a neighbor was,
She got my attention,
By the roses.

CORLENE

1. Corlene is pregnant
    and the consciousness of pregnancy
    comes to me in a dream
    "her labor was hard" I later learn.

    Corlene, in the dream,
    has had her baby,
    and now she is traveling
    on a train
    to rejoin everybody.
    She decides to put the baby back
    inside herself,
    but now he is hard to come out.

    When the baby
    comes out again,
    he is a cat,
    white and black
    and orange
    on different sides
    with a third eye.

2. The cat is taken to a doctor
    to be fixed
    so he becomes human again.

    he grows up to be a boy
    and goes to school.

then, he is playing on a baseball field,
and a kind of radiation hits,
and simultaneously, the government changes
where misfits are not tolerated.
The ray is a kind that causes
cat tendencies to come out.

come out
come out
the cat tendencies come out –
a long striped orange tail
grows out of the boy –
he hides it in his clothes
not to be caught by
the authorities.

suddenly, the boy remembers
his birth
and being called Victor the Cat
when very young
being born
a second time as a cat.

3. I wake up –
    and my friends tell me her labor was hard,
    and that when women are pregnant there is a
    universal cosmic unconscious
    that affects other people,
    that penetrates dreams.

THE LINCOLN PARK NATURAL HISTORY MUSEUM

I once worked in a museum
making exhibits
in a little room
in the basement.
We painted eight hours a day,
what was nature,
real outside,
trying to make it look real.
George, the taxidermist,
had his own shelves
of stuffed animals.
Theo, the Czech artist,
lived in the museum
in his own room
because he could not walk well.
He painted phosphorescent fish
under Black Light –
and to whom Joelle
wrote on a piece of paper,
"Je t'aime, Je t'aime, Je t'aime,"
and slipped it in
front of Theo's hand.
I was kept busy
recreating nature,
remembering to paint shadows,
as though the sun shone inside,
paid at minimal wage,

in the same park
in which I was told
a group of protesters
during the 1968 Democratic Convention
swarmed around
this receptacle
of quiet housing
for glowing painted fish
and stuffed raccoons,
threatening the solitude,
making Lincoln Park
indelibly famous.
In the museum,
life needed to be drawn
to make itself known.
One needed to paint the outside,
not invite it in,
to make the world real.

COFFEEHOUSE

we sit inside a coffeehouse
like we are sitting under
upside down
coffee cups.
we are all waiting
for love.

LUCK

In the Sunnyside,
there are
little houses;
their life flows
like an aquarium
that will bring luck
I was told
from the energy of
the fish swimming.
Living a block from a
tropical fish store
on Monterey Avenue,
the fish's flashing bodies
streak past,
drawing what I perceive
as circles of luck
in a pool of luck
in a world that seems
out of luck.
Yesterday, I told my spouse
there is no luck,
only calculated guesses
but the fish dive deeper
into their submarine world
sending up air to the top.

THE JAPANESE TEA GARDEN

beyond the gates,
the arched bridge
of the tea garden,
my heart totters
on top of it,
reflected in the
water.

HAPPINESS

The little theater company
went to the Salvation Army Seniors
in the Tenderloin
each year,
being offered
the Seniors' lunch
and getting coffee
for ten cents,
with chairs in
three rows for
an audience,
and three chairs
for the actors;
We'd walked past
St. Anthony's food line
and sidewalk
sales of old clothes
to arrive;
Most everyone was Chinese,
some not speaking English,
sometimes a seat mate
would translate;
We liked to be
done by four
to avoid
the twilight street life;
It was usually
our quietest audience,

47

but when
we changed out of
our costumes
and fake beards
and packed up
the props,
one elderly Chinese man,
frail as bamboo,
would say,
"That was very pleasant,"
going up to each one of us,
shaking everyone's hand
in the troupe,
his soft palm,
the consistency of a cloud.

MY BIRTHDAY, DAVID, AND BETTY CARTER

It is my birthday,
a long search for beaches
on a long coast.
Find Betty Carter
in a wrinkle,
a curve,
in the line of
the shore,
turbaned,
low voice, sinking
into the sand or
curving around her
like her bandana.
We sweat
as we watch her
in the summer heat,
run out
to drink lemon soda,
watch the sun
spin around in
her turban,
watch it spin
in the paisley, in orange,
purple, green
and blue swirls,
in hot rings.

JAZZ SILHOUETTE

at Minnie's Can Do Club

shadows on the walls
in the dark core of sound-light
birds fly from our ears
all feet have become flying horses
cigarette smoke covers faces
like a stocking
the music has strings
to pull the walls in
all the walls pulled
to the center
all the shadows lie close
the inside of a rose
dusky smell
a saxophone zips
the chord at center
all music
converged
on one grey point
zips up the night

GRINNELL, 2 A.M.

Flatland sounds
2 a.m. truckers' time
Sher-room on the highway—
C&W on the radio;
blind blanket insomnia
keeps me awake;
clacking traffic lights
direct the empty streets—
puddles reflect stop and go colors;
train whistles blow sharply
to warn the sleeping pedestrians.
Somewhere, someone must be
staring at their ceiling,
watching the night shadows
keep time with the tap-tap
rhythm of the water pipes.
Somewhere, a man and a woman
must be making love to each other
for the first time,
dancing to the body's music,
listening to all the inside sounds.
Darkness invites me into
the belly of a drum.
Just like Jonah
hearing the waves beat against
the whale's hide,
every faucet drip
rolls and resounds
above my head, as though
reverberating over
a stretched skin,
pulled tight.

WINTER'S NOVEL

Been making winter trails
New footprints
In the snow
Can choose any
Direction or tangent
Circles in the clean
Snow,
Until it is lined
And overlapped
And crisscrossed
It looks like
A whole city has
Passed through
This territory,
There are steps to the
    past
There is a cross to go to
    work,
Or a circle of
    play,
The week's novel,
Soft pages of winter.

1. MT. ST. HELENS

Beautiful mountain
lava flow
smoking
blowing demon ash
over land and towns
fueled by rising passion

2. TAHOMA

Rises over the City
with cold serenity
as a God, guardian
cold blue deep unfathomable
clear blue.

WHITE BLOOD CELLS

February, the month of the
first Russian Revolution,
the white blossoms of the plum tree
slowly gain their apex,
three-quarters to their way
to complete beauty,
I wait at the window
and stare at
startling white
as compared to the
loud smaller pink cherry on the street.
February, a shattering
hits the window;
hailing, the white ice
pelts the glass,
hail collecting as
tiny marbles
lacing the yard,
a ghost landscape
beneath the tree
with the white blossoms,
barely a month
before the blossoms
themselves will fall
like soft blowing dancers,
and this scene
of winter and spring
stops me in surprise.
In the evening, after

the hailstorm
there is the poetry reading
that few will go to.
But Jack Hirschman
sits quietly
and speaks sadly
of his son's leukemia,
of white blood cells,
of a mask
of quiet
in the air.

PLUM GATHERING

I never understood
death as the last day,
This was clearer explained to me
by Emily Dickinson
as the carriage that passes by and stops;
time becomes projected
towards tomorrow,
rebounded into next month,
today is a word I ignore,
later I try to count the
hours that I had to give
because I am planting
guilt like into small pots
waiting for greater guilts
to flower;
I do remember
that the plum tree had fruit,
and that each morning
I spent time gathering plums,
picking them from
the tree, and off the
ground – each act
must have taken
a space of minutes,
granting me absolution
in the future
for measuring the time
spent because I

was looking to the future,
not the last moment.
Each plum
turned over,
thrown back,
placed in a basket,
equals a moment that we had,
and each round plum
was sculpted with that
sweet smell,
sunlight and
crushed leaves
of the daily gathering
of plums.

GRANDMA'S SABBATH

The day the tree fell down,
Grandma felt her
own roots shake;
the roots stayed
but the trunk
came down,
upsetting the sky,
creating a strange
falling space
to her ears, deaf.
It was Friday night
so she lit her candles,
she said blessings,
and ate egg bread.
All that death and
dead wood
sweeping past the
windows,
threatening to
crash into the
world of her silent
prayer,
the vibrations
extended into her feet
on her day of rest.
She could feel how God
and the earth
wrestled with each other.

TREE

In December,
I feel my clothed body
as a tree,
parts of me
are ornaments;
my ring,
my shoe,
each layer of
fabric,
wrapping around
adding more
and more
to this
decorated tree –
I, the woman
think of
women decked
with ornaments,
an eyelash,
an eyebrow,
a rouged mouth.
Still, I like myself as this tree
self-conscious,
conspicuous,
glittering sometimes,
akin to the other natural trees
— green and tall —
my ornaments
shine, dance in the sunlight.

SISTER

She who became a
tree this Christmas
planted in the woods
near my home,
the dark Maine woods,
She stayed there
for the whole year,
the snow falling
on her at wintertime,
the rains
beating her branches, her trunk
supporting her in the winds,
her branches like hands and arms
flailing in the storms;
her arms
gather in a picture of fields blown,
cows splattered,
the tops of fences battered;
her needles spill off,
piling on the ground;
the summer dries her out,
makes her green,
makes her stay;
She who became a tree,
She stays with me
in the nearby wood.

HER LAST GIFT

The chimes Kirsten gave us hang on the door,
the blinds down,
I can't see their old rust,
only the shadow sways,
in the sun.
I was going to throw them away,
but the shadows are
too beautiful,
and the sound is still there,
disembodied,
from the solid chimes;
Leave them, leave them,
the birds tell me;
on the porch
only the shadows chime.

POEM TO EMILY

As though no one knew she was a poet,
her poems, hidden in an attic,
no one knew the extent of her.
She so carefully folded her sheets of paper,
carefully found the attic door and tucked them away;
She kneels on the attic boards
piling another thin epistle
wrapping them in ribbons.
Later, feeling their presence above her
and never sending them away
but letting them gather,
nursing each,
like poems hidden in us
waiting in a stack
high above our heads
and she knows they will be found.

THEATER-PIECE

Caught in the folds
Of a curtain
Between stage
And audience
A woman feels
The curtain
Grow hard,
Turn to a
Stone wall,
The wall
   enfolds
      end-folded
       enfolding
Like a frozen
   waterfall,
The woman
A fossil
Now,
Her shell-
Body
About to
Leap or
Flail,
And sitting
In the audience,
People applaud
And wait
For the
Curtains
To part.

ASYLUM

enter this door
it is bronzed and locked.
it tingles when your
fingertips touch it
it is dulled electric
it opens without you having to unlock it
you are behind the door and it is white and transparent
WHITE AND TRANSPARENT
white and transparent
the people behind this door
are white and transparent
they walk on their toes
they have come to this place
they have come to this place
to roll on the ground
    dirt
    shit
    sawdust
    clay
they have come to this place to discover
    the moment of borning
they have come separately looking for hell
they live in dark rooms
they are encompassed in guilt
they run with secret invisible friends
they are rolled into balls of cat fur
the night is their enemy
death is inevitable
they have come to this place
to be healed.

ANSWER: EQUALIZING THE PAIN

having cut myself in the palm
   of one hand
my other hand wants
to be cut, too.
my whole hand
wants to be hurting,
to be aching,
my whole hand wants to be like
   my cut hand
and realizing this, I wonder
why it isn't the cut hand that
wants to be like
   the whole
   one.

BEGINNING TO KNOW FREEDOM

so used to bumps,
I bump myself to feel
old aches,
I cherish these aches,
stuffing them into
weighty knapsacks
that I lug on my
back.

oh freedom,
why erect four walls
in a round
world,
oh freedom,
I have just begun
to know you,
oh freedom, I reach
out to touch
you,
  aglow,
   aglow,
  aglow.

RESIDUES OF FEELING

Like the last drops of paint
on the palette, the
easel, the water
color brush, a little
feeling stays;
I dip into the color
on occasions,
paint it on tiny
canvasses,
wash the brushes and
watch the remaining
color wash
away. This urge to
paint comes at the
oddest of times.
Sketching memories,
the collected residues
of feeling
becoming more
transparent, thinner
with each brush stroke.
One day all those colors
will become less and
less decipherable,
more water than paint, or
blood, or feelings.

THE ANARCHIST BOOKSTORE ON HAIGHT STREET

The door of the Anarchist Bookstore
is not always open.
Now the door is closed
against the chill rain,
and the corners
are filled with ghosts.
The waiters, outside on a stoop,
discuss books for a moment
(we are all strangers to each other)
and read hand-scribbled signs
that announce workers' holidays and strikes.
At last, a time having arrived, the door opens,
and the door closes;
inside Tet sits softly behind the desk
tapping messages to anarchist greats.
Tet says some people take magazines
but then the magazines reappear
because the magazines have been brought back.
So, I ask myself,
what are the limits of my anarchy?

FORTY-THREE

The year that I am forty-three,
the forty-three bus line is my closest bus.
This bus turns its corner
and begins its ascent
past Joe's Broiler
into the hills,
around houses like ones I left
in the suburbs,
houses with rose gardens
and children with book bags and bicycles,
my fifteen years of living in the city
rushing by me
as the bus swerves
and the travelers change
from the older ladies
who still wear white gloves
to the teenagers
in the bus' back
who get on at Ninth Avenue,
the bus finally connecting me
to the Haight Ashbury.
This year I am forty-three
like this bus
that throws everyone
off-balance on
each turn of the road.

1967 AND SENIOR YEAR IN HIGH SCHOOL

It was held in the gymnasium,
not the auditorium,
on bleachers,
almost like a sports event,
a man came to tell us
not to take drugs,
it was 1967,
but it was not only
drugs he was against,
he warned us
against Allen Ginsberg,
the homosexual author,
everything that Ginsberg stood for,
the man shouted out like a drill Sergeant,
was I the only one
who wondered why
he could say all the
things he was saying?
Three thousand of us
left the gym
through the two doors,
and as I got to the door
wanting air,
a high school boy
fell down on the
tan gym floor,
three feet from my feet,
twisting and kicking,
having an epileptic seizure,

70

in front of the entire student body,
filing by him,
in threes and fours,
a student body of
three thousand students,
all of our eyes were
fixed on his form
for a moment.
It was my Senior Year in High School,
and all I wanted was to write poetry
like Allen Ginsberg
and to keep moving
into the air.

THE EXTERMINATOR'S VISIT

The mice hide behind their
pockets in the walls.
The roaches make
decorative patches
in the kitchen,
"Things" that I don't
tell many people about.
Thursday is the scheduled day
for the Exterminator's visit,
a line of white powder
and that now-grown
familiar smell
goes around the bottom
of the room
and inhabits the
whole building,
poisoned mice disappear,
making my room empty
except for the strange uncertainty,
and the strange relief,
I feel that it could all be worse,
or maybe it will be;
the woman across the hall
fills her room
with hanging plants,
maybe it is what makes her
room filled,
while mine is so empty;
sometimes I elect

not to have the exterminator
except I feel guilty about my roaches
walking into other apartments
and he is talkative and nice,
making me, against my judgment,
enjoy his visits;
maybe it will be worse
in five years
when all the poisons settle,
but these feelings pass
on the next day
until a month later
when "things"
and the exterminator
reappear.
After I move from the building,
the company's landlords stopped having
the exterminator come,
and for four months
there was a rent strike
at the building.
But I had moved on
to questioning
other environments,
— paints and smokes and people,
because there is so much that
is slightly toxic,
because there are
so many "things"
that one does not
wish to speak about.

SIGHT/INSIGHT

Inside the shadows,
the spaces be-
tween the
grey, the
tingling light,
the numbness
of white on
white paper,
the reflection
of leaves on
paper
      inside
the shadows,
the innocent
traces of
unformed
pictures,
little amoebic
bodies
fluctuating
swelling out
to their limits.

GRANDPA HARRY'S ARMCHAIR

One word –
you could turn
it around,
make a whole
world out of it,
or two, because
the words could
be turned
upside down.
He would explain
very carefully
what a Yiddish word
meant in English,
its meaning
could encompass
hours, days.
I was very small
in the big brown
armchair,
and the words
were big.

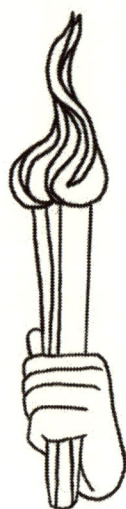

ABOUT THE AUTHOR

Alice Elizabeth Rogoff lives in San Francisco. She has been an Editor of the *Haight Ashbury Literary Journal* since 1984. She has a BA in Anthropology from Grinnell College, Masters Degrees in English: Concentration Creative Writing and in Drama from San Francisco State University, and a Certificate in Labor Studies from City College San Francisco. She has been published in *Poetry At The 33*, *The San Francisco Bark – A Gathering of Bay Area Poets*, *Borderlands – Texas Poetry Review*, *The Small Pond Magazine of Literature*, *Beat (Poetry and Arts)*, and *The Noe Valley Voice*. She received an Honorable Award in the Artists Embassy International Dance-Poem Contest. She is on the Steering Committee of the National Writers Union Bay Area chapter. She is the Recording Secretary for the San Francisco Living Wage Coalition, and leads drama workshops for low-income adults.

Photograph by Howard Pflanzer

ANTHOLOGY PUBLICATIONS

Poetry At The 33

The San Francisco Bark – A Gathering of Bay Area Poets

Noe Valley – An Anthology of Poetry

Quasar

It's All Good

The View from Here

Alice E. Rogoff
c/o 1st World Library
PO Box 2211
Fairfield, Iowa 52556
alicerogoff@yahoo.com

Printed in the United States

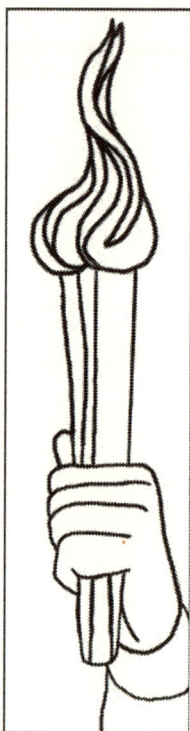

www.ingramcontent.com/pod-product-compliance
Lightning Source LLC
Chambersburg PA
CBHW032024090426
42741CB00006B/732